This book belongs to

. . . .

. . . .

My Favourite Bible Stories

William Collins
An imprint of HarperCollinsPublishers
1 London Bridge Street
London SE1 9GF

WilliamCollinsBooks.com

First published in Great Britain by William Collins in 2020

1

A catalogue record for this book is available from the British Library

ISBN 978-000-836542-4

Text by Sarah Fletcher

Printed and bound in China

My Favourite Bible Stories

Illustrated by Kelly-Jade Nicholls

Stories by Sarah Fletcher

Collins

SINCE 1819

This Big Book

This big book tells the *greatest story* ever!

It's all about **God** and **us** but the story could be called,
"GOD'S GREAT RESCUE!"

The story begins *way, way back* and there are **lots** of people
to find in the pages and lots of things that happen.

So, are you ready to discover the story
and have a good look?

Well, let's get going and *open the book!*

To the grown-ups!

Welcome to *My Favourite Bible Stories*!

This book is a storytelling journey through many much-loved Bible stories. It is written with fun, rhythm and a splash of gentle rhyme to help bring these amazing stories to life for your young reader.

The book is a vibrant telling of the Biblical stories and not a direct translation of scripture. It seeks to be true to the feel and message of Biblical accounts but there are scripture references through the pages if you wish to explore the original narratives in a deeper way.

With each story there is something to think about with your little one, something to do together and something your child can pray if they would like to.

Our longing is that children will love reading the stories and discover through them THE RESCUER.

We hope that you and your little one love dipping into these stories together!

From Kelly-Jade and Sarah

 # Contents

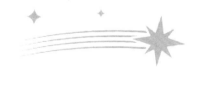

In the Very Beginning

Genesis 1:1-31, 2:1-3

In the very beginning, before anything HOPPED or SQUEAKED on the earth, there was **God.**

God looked at the emptiness all around and smiled, "I know! It's time to make something wonderful. Ready, steady, go!"

Day 1

First, God spoke into the deep, deep dark and said, "LIGHT!"

Suddenly, with a FLASH and a *SPARK,* brilliant white BLAZED out bright. God laughed and said, "It's a really good sight! I'll call the light, **'day'** and the darkness, **'night'**!"

Day 2

God breathed in deep, closed his eyes, and then breathed out a little word, "Sky!" And there, in a thousand brush-strokes of blue, the **heavens** were painted wide and high.

Day 3

God spoke with a low rumble in his voice and rich brown soil TUMBLED into **land**. With a SPLASH of blue and SPLISH of green, **salty sea** crashed over the sand.

Next, God had a think, and began to plant greens, yellows, reds and pink. **Flowers** and **trees** sprung up from the ground like a sweet smelling garden with fruit all around.

Day 4

Now it was time for something fun, something called **"moon"** and something called **"sun"**. God THREW lights into space and time, leaving **stars** to SPARKLE and TWINKLE and SHINE.

Day 5

God looked at the earth and loved what he saw, but still He wanted to make some more. So, with a SQUAWK and a FLAP, a SWISH and a SPLISH, the earth was filled with **birds** and **fish**.

Day 6

With a fluff of fur and pad of paw, with spots and stripes and patterns galore, with S C U T T L E and STOMP, BOING, BOUNCE and C R A W L , God made the **animals** big and small!

Lastly God took a handful of dust saying, "Let's make **friends** just like us!" He breathed His breath in the people made of clay, and they started to DANCE and LAUGH and PLAY.

He gave them His garden so they could have fun and God's story with us had just begun.

And on the seventh day God had a rest!

Have a think

God is the great artist. He made an amazing world for us to share and look after. He made us so that we could enjoy being friends with Him!

Have a go

Can you paint a picture of our beautiful world? What kind of plants and animals will you have in your painting?

Have a pray

Dear God, Thank you that you made everything and you made me. You really are the greatest artist. Amen.

A Big Bite

Genesis 2:4-25, 3:1-24

God made a man called *Adam* and a woman called *Eve.* God *loved* them and they were His *friends.*

God gave them EVERYTHING in His garden, except **one** thing. He said, "My friends, ***don't*** eat the fruit from the tree of the knowledge of good and evil. ***Trust me,*** if you eat it you will die. *Everything* else is yours to try!"

Adam and Eve lived happily in the garden, *close to God* and *close to each other.*

But then, God's *enemy* called the devil, came to RUIN this perfect world. He took on the shape of a *snake* and SLITHERED up to Eve smirking, "Sssss! Did God really say that you can't eat from any of these lovely trees? How *mean! Sssss!*"

Eve said, "No, we can eat from all of them except one. If we eat from it we'll die."

The sneaky snake HISSED, "You won't die! God is telling you lies! He knows that if you eat it you will become very *wise* about good and evil. The fruit is really tasty, why not have a try? *Ssss!*"

The fruit did *seem* good, so Eve took A BIG BITE. MUNCH, MUNCH, CRUNCH, CRUNCH. The fruit was nice, the snake must have been right! Eve gave some to Adam and he took A BIG BITE. MUNCH, MUNCH, CRUNCH, CRUNCH. The snake SNIGGERED at the sight.

As soon as they had eaten, they realised they were naked. Then they felt **ashamed** for what they had done and they tried to HIDE from God.

God called out, "Adam, my friend, where are you?" Adam was afraid and stammered, "Um, we're over here, hiding away."

Then it all came out, how the snake had *tricked* them and without a doubt they had *listened* to the *story* he had *spun*. They had *ignored* what God, their friend, had told them and the GREAT SEPARATION had begun.

Their friendship with God had been TORN APART, they had to leave the garden and *God's* **heart** was broken for the ones he loved. Now they would *KNOW* what sadness *was all about*, for *death* and *evil* had been sown into the once perfect world.

Yet God would never abandon those he had made and he already *had a plan* through which *everything* could change. He would send THE RESCUER to make the way. THE RESCUER who would right the wrongs. THE RESCUER who would *save the day.*

Have a think

Adam and Eve made a really bad choice in the garden. They chose to go their own way and ignore God. In that moment friendship with God was broken and pain and sadness came into the world. But God always loved people and was always planning a great rescue so everyone could be close to him again.

Have a go

Tell your grown-up about a time when you have ignored a warning that someone who loves you has given. How does it affect things when you have chosen not to listen?

Have a pray

Dear God, Thank you that even though things looked really bad, you were always planning a great rescue for the world. Amen.

Noah's Boat

Genesis 6:1-9:17

Many years later the people of the earth had *turned against* God and *turned against* each other. God was *sad* because everyone was so full of **HATE.** Everyone that is, except **Noah**. So God was planning a great rescue, where He would save Noah and make everything new.

God said, "Noah, my friend, you need to build a *really big boat* so when the earth is flooded your family and the animals will stay afloat!"

Noah began to build with a TAP, TAP, TAP and a TAT, TAT, TAT. Wood on wood and nail on nail soon Noah's Ark was ready to sail.

Next, with a STOMP and a SCUTTLE, a HOP and a FLAP, a SNORT, an OINK, a BAAA and a MOO. All types of animals came to the Ark and climbed on board *two by two.*

The animals came on board two by two.

When Noah and his family were *safe* inside, God shut the big wooden door. And then the rain began to POUR AND POUR…

With a PITTER PATTER, CLITTER CLATTER, PLIP, PLOP, P L O P, for forty days and forty nights the pelting rain just did not stop! The floodwaters rose right up to the sky but all in the Ark were *safe and dry!*

A boat afloat on the flooded earth! It must have been quite a sight. But Noah trusted God to keep them *SAFE*, he fed the animals and sat tight.

Until eventually the rain stopped and God started to blow the floodwaters away.

Noah sent a dove to search for land and it flew back carrying a *leaf,* for the trees were beginning to *poke* and *peak* above the waters high and soon the land would all be *dry.*

After many days and many nights the Ark landed on a solid mound. Everyone came out of the boat and walked on **dry ground.** Hooray!

Noah said, "Thank you, God, for *keeping us SAFE.* Help us to live close to you all of our days."

God promised he would **never** flood the whole earth again and he put the *rainbow* in the *sky,* as a sign of PEACE and LOVE DIVINE.

So when you see the colourful bow with its *red, orange, yellow, green, blue, violet* and *indigo,* remember that God **loves** us and will never leave us on our own.

Have a think

God rescued Noah, his family and the animals. He kept them safe and gave them a chance to start again.

Have a go

Collect some pebbles or bottle tops and paint each one as a different animal, or as the different people in Noah's family. Get a small box and paint it like a boat. Now, put everyone safe and sound in the Ark!

Have a pray

Dear God, Thank you that you love us and that you have promised to always be with us. Amen.

A Sky Full of Stars

Genesis 12:1-9, 15:1-6, 21:1-7

Years later God spotted a man called Abraham and whispered to him, "Come on a **great adventure** with Me!" God *promised* He would give Abraham and his wife Sarah a place to call *home.* So, they set out *not knowing* where they were going but *knowing* that the God who made everything was **with them**.

Along the way, they became *friends* with God and got to know him. But Abraham and Sarah had a ***deep sadness*** in their hearts. They didn't have a *baby* and they really *wished* they did!

Abraham and Sarah got *older* and *older, way too old* to have a child. But one day God said, "Abraham, my friend, don't be afraid, I am the one who looks after you. I am your ***great treasure.***" Abraham sighed, "I know, God, but the thing I really desire, is not possible. I don't have a child and I'm now old."

But God said, "You and Sarah *will* have a *son*. **I promise!**" Then God took Abraham outside and whispered, "Look up at the stars and count them one by one."

Abraham looked at **a sky full of stars** that GLISTENED and GLIMMERED and SPARKLED and SHONE.

And he started to count, "1, 2, 3, 4, 5..." but there were so many stars his head soon spun! God said, "That's how many your *children, grandchildren, great grandchildren, great great grandchildren* will be. And I will be their friend too."

It was impossible! But Abraham BELIEVED what God had said.

Years passed and still Sarah had no baby. They were getting *older* and *older* but God had **promised** and God had *not forgotten.*

Then when Sarah was *ninety-one* and Abraham was *one hundred*, Sarah felt a KICK in her tummy. A new little life was MOVING. A new baby was GROWING bigger and bigger and bigger! It all happened, *just as God had said.*

When the baby was born, WAH, WAH, WAH, they called him Isaac. And Sarah laughed and cried saying, "God has *remembered* me. God has turned my sadness into **laughter.** God is so very kind."

And they held their GIGGLING, WRIGGLING son in their wrinkled hands and *thanked* God for all that He had done.

Have a think

God was with Abraham and Sarah and had good plans for their lives. He remembered His promises to them and gave them hope for the future. It was through Abraham's family that THE RESCUER would one day come.

Have a go

At night-time look out of your window and count any stars you can see. How do you think Abraham felt looking at all the stars and hearing God's promise to him?

Have a pray

Dear God, Thank you that you are with me and have good things planned for my life. Thank you that nothing is impossible for you and you remember what you have promised. Amen.

Something Beautiful

Genesis 24:1-67

Baby Isaac grew up and owned lots of things, but he was **lonely.** He didn't have a *special person* to *love.*

Abraham knew that God who had *guided* him all his life would *make the way* for his son to find a lovely wife. So, Abraham sent his servant back to where his relatives lived to look for someone special for Isaac.

When he got to a spring of water the servant *prayed*, "God of Abraham, please *guide* me *today*! May the girl who offers me water and *also* offers to give water to my camels, be the *one* you are thinking of for Abraham's son." Just then, a girl came to the spring.

The servant said to her, "Please can I have some water?" The girl had a kind heart and said, "Oh yes, of course and I'll draw water for your camels too!" The servant couldn't believe his ears and watched to see what the girl would do.

The girl gave him a drink and then got water for ALL his camels.

There were a *lot* of camels and camels can drink a *lot* of water! SPLISH, SPLASH, GUZZLE, GUZZLE, SPLISH, SPLASH, GUZZLE, GUZZLE, SPLISH!

When the camels had finished drinking the servant asked, "What is your family *name*?" It turned out they were from the very *same* family as Abraham! The girl was called Rebekah and Abraham was her great uncle! God had led the servant *straight* to Abraham's people! It was a miracle!

Then the servant told Rebekah's parents the *whole story.* He said, "God has *heard* Abraham's prayer and my prayer too. God has led me straight to you!" He asked if Rebekah would go back with him to marry Isaac, for that is how things were done in those days. Rebekah smiled and said, "Yes, I will go. It feels like God is guiding us, so we can leave *straight away*." And they set out.

One evening as they got near Abraham's home, Rebekah saw Isaac walking across the fields heading *their way*. And there, under another *sky full of stars* the two of them met and the rest, as they say, is history!

And Isaac really did love Rebekah. She was the special person his heart was longing for. God had *guided* them both into something beautiful.

Have a think

God was writing a miracle love story for Isaac and Rebekah. God loves to guide us in the small and big things of life and He has good stories for us to live.

Have a go

Try and guess how much water a camel can drink. Do some research with your grown-up to discover the answer!

Rebekah must have spent ages getting all that water, she really was very kind!

Have a pray

Dear God, Thank you that you love to guide me and you have good stories for me to live. Amen.

Jacob the Trickster

Genesis 25:19-34, 27:1-33:20

Isaac and Rebekah had twin boys, Esau and Jacob. They did *NOT* get on and Jacob was a bit of a trickster!

One time, Jacob *tricked* Esau out of his birth-right. Another time, he *fooled* his own dad into giving *him* the blessing of goodness that was meant for his *brother!*

Esau was FURIOUS about it all and wanted to kill Jacob. So Jacob ran a **long, looong, loooong** way away!

On his journey Jacob had a dream…

In the dream Jacob saw a ***special stairway*** bridging the HUGE **gap** between *heaven and earth*, the **gap** between *God and man.* And on that stairway God smiled and said, "I am the God of Abraham and Isaac, let's be **friends.** *I am with you* and the whole world will be blessed through you."

Jacob woke up saying, "Wow! *God Almighty is actually here with me!*"

....

Jacob finally got to his uncle's house and there he fell *deeply* in love with Rachel, AHHHH! But his uncle Laban was a *trickster* just like Jacob. When it was Jacob and Rachel's wedding day Laban *switched* Rachel with her older sister, Leah, and *fooled* Jacob into marrying her. Jacob was NOT happy!

Jacob eventually married both sisters, which was normal in those days, and Jacob had lots of children! WAH, WAH, WAH!
1, 2, 3, 4, 5, 6, 7, 8, 9, 10, 11, 12...
Twelve sons!

Eventually, Jacob decided it was time to go home. He sent a message to his brother Esau and then sent lots of gifts, hoping to *make peace* with him. Jacob sent sheep, BAAA, goats, MAAA, camels, CHEW, cows, MOOO, bulls,

SNORT and donkeys too, *EEEorre!*

....

Just before he met Esau, Jacob was all on his own. It was night and God, in the shape of a man, *wrestled* with him.

Jacob the trickster had fought with people *all his life* but now he needed *peace with God*. Jacob said to the God-man, "I won't let you go until *you* bless me with your favour and peace." Jacob did not give up and so God said, "I'm going to *change your name* from 'Jacob' to 'Israel' and you'll be *different* from today."

As the morning sun peeped over the hills, the God-man left. Jacob realised he had been wrestling with God and gasped, "I have seen God *face to face*! God is so *kind* that he wants to be *my* friend!" Jacob had finally made peace with God.

Then Jacob and Esau met, they *made peace* with each other and they became friends.

God *changed* Jacob from being a *trickster* to becoming someone who *brought good* on the earth. Out of his family the whole nation of Israel would come. Out of Israel, THE RESCUER would one day be born. THE RESCUER who would **bridge the gap** between God and man, THE RESCUER for everyone.

Have a think

Jacob was a trickster but God wanted to bridge the gap between them, give Jacob a fresh start and help him change.

Have a go

Can you build a bridge out of blocks? Start from both sides and build towards the middle. Can you find a way to bridge the gap right in the centre?

Have a pray

Dear God, Thank you that you can help anyone change. You love to give us all a fresh start. Amen.

Joseph the Dreamer

Genesis 37:1-36

Joseph was Jacob's FAVOURITE son and Jacob gave him a *colourful coat* to prove it. Joseph SWISHED and SWIRLED in the special coat, *yellow* as the sun, *red* as the berries, *blue* as the sky. It made his brothers MAD! They GRUMBLED, "Who does this *runt* think he is!"

Then to make things worse, Joseph had *strange dreams.* In the dreams he saw bundles of corn and then the stars, moon and sun all *BOWING DOWN* to **him.** Joseph SWIRLED and gloated, "I've had some dreams and they clearly show that one day **you,** my brothers, will **all bow** to ME. What fun!" The brothers GROWLED, they had had *enough* of this *favourite* son!

One day Jacob sent Joseph to check on his brothers who were looking after the sheep, BAAA! But the *brothers* spotted him and began to *scheme.* "This is our chance!" said one brother, "Let's do away with this multi-coloured dreamer!" Reuben said, "No! Don't take his blood. Let's just throw him in this pit, that will be enough!" for Reuban planned to rescue Joseph later.

Like a pack of wolves hungry to POUNCE, the brothers GRABBED Joseph. They RIPPED off his *colourful coat* and THREW him into the deep echoey hole, WHEEEE...PLOP! OH NO!

Joseph shouted, *"Hello o o. Please ease ease. Help elp elp. Me e e!"* But the brothers walked away.

Just then traders heading to Egypt LOLLOPED by on their camels. The brothers had an idea, "Let's *sell* the boy!" they gleefully said. And that is what they did!

When Reuben came back to the pit to pull Joseph out, he wasn't there! Reuben wailed, "The boy has gone! What shall we do now?"

So, the brothers took the RAGGED TATTERS of Joseph's coat, DIPPED it in animal blood and carried it to their dad saying, "We found this!" Jacob cried, "Joseph must have been *torn* to pieces by wild animals. My *favourite son* has died!"

Jacob's heart was broken over his MUCH LOVED son. But little did he know that Joseph's *story* had just begun.

Have a think

The dreams Joseph had about his life were actually from God, for God had chosen him for a special purpose. But the journey that was needed for those dreams to come about was only just beginning.

Have a go

Collage a picture of Joseph's colourful coat. How many colours can you use?

Have a pray

Dear God, Thank you that you have dreams for my life. Please help me know that you are with me on the journey. Amen.

Joseph in Egypt

Genesis 39:1-41:49

Joseph was SOLD as a SLAVE to Potiphar... **and the days went by.**

But in Potiphar's house, Joseph *worked hard* and he earned Potiphar's trust.

Joseph was handsome, Joseph was smart and it wasn't long before Potiphar's wife *smoothly* said, "Come to bed with me, no one will know!" But Joseph *kept* on saying, "NO!" Until one day she *grabbed* him by his clothes, Joseph ran away but she told a horrible lie and wailed, "Joseph has attacked me!" Potiphar was MAD and threw Joseph in jail!

The door was SLAMMED SHUT... and the days went by.

But in prison, Joseph kept on *working hard* and he *listened* to God. So, when Pharaoh's Cupbearer and Baker had STRANGE

DREAMS, Joseph said, "God alone understands dreams, so I'll tell you what they mean." The Cupbearer's dream meant freedom, HOORAY. The Baker's dream meant death, UH OH! And the dreams *came true* just like Joseph had said. The Cupbearer promised to remember Joseph when he was free, but then he *forgot immediately!*

For two more years Joseph WAITED in jail... and the days went by.

But Joseph stayed *faithful* and stayed *trusting* in God. Until one day **Pharaoh** himself had STRANGE DREAMS that *no one* could understand. The Cupbearer suddenly remembered Joseph and said, "There is a man in prison who will be able to help." So in a blink, Joseph went from the prison to the *palace.*

Pharaoh asked, "Can you tell me what my dreams mean?" Joseph shook his head, "I can't, but God will. Tell me your dreams."

Pharaoh said, "I saw the seven *fattest* cows you ever have seen, GOBBLED right up by seven *scrawny* cows. It was really very mean and those seven *skinny* cows were all *gangly* and *lean*, URGHHH." Then… "I saw seven golden ears of juicy ripe corn, GOBBLED right up by seven *scrawny* ears. There was nothing of the good corn left at all and the **scraggly** ears were so *ragged* and *small*, URGHHH!"

What could the strange dreams mean?

Joseph said, "The two dreams mean the **same** thing. There will be **seven good years** in Egypt where there will be lots of food. But then there will be **seven bad years** of famine. So, you should find a wise person to collect food in the *good years* that will help Egypt through the *bad years*. Pharaoh nodded and said, "Good idea, I think the wisest person is YOU!"

And Pharaoh made Joseph **second in charge**. ALL of Egypt did what he said. He gathered food in the *good years* so that Egypt was ready for the *bad years* ahead.

Joseph ruled wisely and faithfully… and the days went by.

And all the time, God was working out a *grand plan* to RESCUE many.

Have a think

Joseph's story seemed to go from bad to worse. But God was with him in all the hard days. Joseph was learning and growing and God was always planning to turn things around to help many.

Have a go

Can you pretend to be grand Pharaoh telling Joseph his strange dreams? Can you think of different ways to describe the cows and ears of corn?

Have a pray

Dear God, Thank you that you are always with me, even in the hard days. Please help me learn and grow and always know that you are working out a good plan. Amen.

Hooray for Joseph!

Genesis 42:1–47:31

The seven years passed and then *famine* hit HARD and WIDE. Until everyone's bellies *rumbled inside!* The people were *starving*, their faces were thin, their stomachs popped and their legs buckled in! And so Joseph *gave out* the food he'd stored in the seven good years. Egypt was RESCUED and with tears in their eyes they all shouted, "HOORAY FOR JOSEPH!"

But the famine GOBBLED up food everywhere, even for Joseph's own family.

So, Jacob sent his sons to buy grain from the *ruler of Egypt*. And Joseph's **dreams** *started to come true.*

One day *Joseph's brothers* turned up in Pharaoh's land and got down on their knees and hands before Joseph. They didn't seem to recognise him but they were all bowing down, *just like in his dreams!*

Joseph pretended to be angry and called them, "SPIES!" The brothers shook their heads saying, "We're not telling lies" But Joseph put them in prison, CLANG, and then sent *all but one* home, telling them to *bring back* Benjamin the youngest son to prove who they were.

Jacob didn't want to let Benjamin go, but after a while he couldn't say no because there *wasn't any* food *anywhere.* So the brothers *and* Benjamin went back to Pharaoh's land and they ALL bowed before Joseph on their knees and hands.

When Joseph saw Benjamin, his very OWN younger brother, he started to CRY as he remembered all that had happened and all the questions of *why?* Still he didn't let them know who he was. He gave them *sacks of food* but hid a SILVER CUP in Benjamin's grain, for he wanted to see if his brothers were the *same* as all those years ago.

As soon as the brothers had left the palace, Joseph sent *soldiers* demanding, "WHO has stolen the *silver chalice,* whoever has it will become our *slave for life.*" It was of course found in Benjamin's sack and the soldiers dragged them back to stand in front of *Egypt's ruler.* And then something happened that showed

Joseph his *brothers* had really *changed…* Judah offered *his own life* in Benjamin's place!

Joseph whispered, "Brothers, come close. *It's me Joseph!* Don't be afraid. What you meant for harm all those years ago, God has *used for good* so that MANY lives could be saved!"

The brothers couldn't believe their *ears* but their *eyes* told them it was true. Joseph was ruler of Egypt and he had *forgiven* them through and through!

Joseph sent for his dad and when they *hugged,* their hearts were glad. So, Jacob, the brothers and all their families lived in Egypt to escape the famine that was still to come.

Joseph had RESCUED *each* and *every single one.*

Have a think

The dreams Joseph had for his life when he was young were really from God. It took a long time, but eventually they came true. The dreamer became a rescuer for many people.

Have a go

Joseph forgave his brothers even though they'd really hurt him. Is there anyone who has hurt you that you can forgive? Spend a bit of time talking to God about it, asking Him to help you and asking Him to turn things around for good.

Have a pray

Dear God, Thank you that you are always looking for ways to bring good, even out of bad situations. Thank you that you know how to bring dreams to pass. Amen.

Moses - What a Surprise!

Exodus 1:1-2:10

Jacob's family had grown bigger and bigger until there were loads of them in Egypt. The years passed and a new Pharaoh came to power, one who didn't know anything about Joseph.

So the Egyptians started to *hate* Jacob's people, who were now known as Israel's people or the Hebrews. They turned them into *slaves* and *forced* them to work under the **hot, hot, Egyptian sun** making *brick after brick, tower after tower, city after city.*

The people were EXHAUSTED and *cried out* to God to RESCUE them.

Pharaoh's heart was as *hard as stone* and he didn't want any more children of Israel in his land, so, he *ordered* that all the Hebrew baby boys should be *killed!*

But during this time a little Hebrew baby boy was born, WAH, WAH, WAH! His parents *loved* him and didn't want him to die, so they came up with a *plan*.

His mum took a basket and *painted* it in *sticky tar* to make it *waterproof.* She put her *sleeping baby* inside and **trusted** him to the **God who saves.** Then she put the boat-basket on the river. The baby's sister, Miriam, ran along the riverbank to see where the basket would go...

It went down the *winding river* and the boat-basket BOB, BOB, BOBBED along.

It went around the ***twists*** and ***turns*** and the baby-basket BOB, BOB, BOBBED along.

It went all the way to a clump of reeds where Pharaoh's daughter was having a bath and the sleeping baby BOB, BOB, BOBBED along. And then the *baby* woke up, "WAH, WAH, WAH!" Pharaoh's daughter opened the basket to see what was inside... *"WAH, WAH, WAH!"*

"What a surprise!" she gasped, "It's one of the Hebrew baby boys. Isn't he *cute*!"

Pharaoh's daughter lifted the little baby out of the basket-boat and ROCKED him gently in her arms till he went, "WAH, WHA, AH, AH, SNORE, SNORE, SNORE!"

Pharaoh's daughter fell in *love* with the baby and decided to keep

Pharaoh's daughter opened the basket to see what was inside.

him. The baby's sister offered to find a Hebrew woman to nurse the baby and Pharaoh's daughter said, "What a good idea!" So, Miriam went to get her *own* mum who then nursed her *own* baby boy as he grew up in Pharaoh's *own* household!

Pharaoh's daughter called the baby **Moses** and God was *with him*. For God had HEARD his people's cries and He was planning a G R E A T RESCUE.

Have a think

Things looked really bad for Israel's people but God was planning their rescue and had a special part for Moses to play in the story.

Years later, God would send THE RESCUER for everyone.

Have a go

Take a wooden washing peg and paint a baby's face at one end, then wrap cloth around the rest of the baby. Now take a cardboard tube and with your grown-up's help, cut a rectangle in one of the sides. Paint the tube brown like a boat and then pop the baby in the boat-basket.

Have a pray

Dear God, Thank you that you always hear our cry and you are the great RESCUER. Amen.

Moses and Pharaoh

Exodus 2:11-12:42

Moses grew up in Pharaoh's palace but he knew it wasn't fair for his own people to be treated so badly under the *glare* of the **hot, hot Egyptian sun.** One day Moses saw an Egyptian *hitting* an Israelite slave and so he *hit* the Egyptian. The Egyptian died and Moses ran away.

Moses then spent forty years in the desert!

But God **hadn't forgotten** him and God **hadn't forgotten** His people.

One day Moses saw a bush that was SPARKING and SIZZLING with *FLAMES* but the bush *didn't* burn up, it just stayed the same. Moses took a closer look and God spoke to him out of that bush saying, "Moses, I AM WITH YOU and I have heard my people's cry. Now go and tell Pharaoh that it's *freedom time* for the Israelites!"

Moses was really *scared,* after all he'd made a *big* mistake when he was young. Why would the Hebrew people, or Pharaoh, listen to what he had to say! But God **promised** He was with him and sent his brother Aaron to help on the way.

So, Moses and Aaron went to Pharaoh with trembling knees and said, "Please, the God of Israel says, '**Let my people go!**'" But Pharaoh said, "NO". And then he made the Israelites work even harder under the **hot, hot, Egyptian sun**.

The people were angry with Moses and Moses didn't know what to do. But God had a RESCUE PLAN that would bring them all through to *freedom*. So He sent Moses back to Pharaoh with the message, "Let my people go!" But Pharaoh's heart was hard and he still said, "NO!"

So then God sent *plagues* upon the Egyptians, for God *hated* the slavery and wanted his people to live in *liberty*. Every time Pharaoh refused to let the people go, a plague would hit hard until the hearts of the Egyptians *slowly* began to change.

In the final plague, *Death's dark shadow* crept across the land. But the Israelites were told to put the *blood of a lamb* on their door as a sign for death to *pass over* them and not to go near any of their firstborn.

That night there was a lot of sadness in Egypt as their own firstborn sons died, but the Israelites were kept COMPLETELY SAFE. Now Pharaoh wanted the Hebrews gone. AT LAST, it was their **freedom day!**

Hooray!

Have a think

Moses had made some mistakes when he was young. But God still had a plan for his life and wanted to use him to help bring many to freedom.

Have a go

Stick some twigs on a piece of paper. Now either use paint or tissue paper to create a picture of the burning bush.

Have a pray

Dear God, Thank you that you always have a plan to rescue and to help. Thank you that you are with me and can use me to help others even if I have made mistakes in the past. Amen.

Moses and the Great Rescue

Exodus 13:17-14:31

The Israelites headed out of Egypt and out of slavery. They CHEERED and DANCED... until they got to the **Red Sea.** For then Pharaoh *changed his mind!* He didn't want to lose all his slaves so he sent his *army* to find them and bring them back again.

The sea was in front of them and the Egyptians behind. The *sea stretched far* and the *army wide* and the people were **terrified.** BUT GOD WAS WITH THEM.

God told Moses to hold his stick over the sea and watch how God would bring the victory.

All through the night God caused a *strong wind* to BLOW and the water TUMBLED and CRASHED aside with a WHOOSH. God *held back* the *pounding sea* and PARTED the waves with a 1, 2, 3.

Walls of water were held up on both sides and the people walked THROUGH the sea on a path that was *dry*. God was fighting for his people and now the Egyptians were **terrified!**

But Pharaoh *ordered* the army to go after them. So, God let the waters fall back to the ground. They ROARED, *RACED* and TUMBLED around the Egyptian army until the army were *washed away*.

The Hebrew people were ALL SAFE!

GOD THE RESCUER had saved the day. Now the people could live in *freedom* as *friends of God*. He would *always* be with them and He would guide their way.

Hooray, Hooray, Hooray!

Have a think

This was a great rescue. The people were brought out of slavery into freedom, where they could walk closely with God and be his special friends. In a similar way, God would later send THE RESCUER to make the way for us all to be free and to be his friends.

Have a go

Paint the outside of a jam jar blue, you could paint some little fish on the outside too. When the paint is dry, look into the jar and imagine it is the tunnel of water that the people of Israel walked through.

Have a pray

Dear God, Thank you that you are the great RESCUER and you want to give us freedom so we can walk closely with you and be your friend. Amen.

Joshua and Jericho

Joshua 1:1-11, 6:1-21

Moses led God's people for many years, teaching them what it meant to live as *friends of God.* Sometimes the people got it *right* and sometimes they got it *really wrong.* But God was always **with them** and *promised* them a place to call **home.**

When Moses died, Joshua became their leader. Joshua had known God since he was little and now God gave him the BIG job of leading the people into the land He had promised them. But there were many enemies to fight along the way and many cities to win.

Joshua felt *small* and was afraid because the job was SO BIG. But God *promised,* "Joshua my friend, be STRONG and COURAGEOUS for I am **with you.**"

The first city they got to was Jericho.

It had HIGH walls and TALL towers with no way in and no way out. Joshua didn't know *how* to win the city but God had a *plan*. And it seemed quite a strange one!

Joshua and the Israelite army were to *march* around the city once each day for *six* days, but they were not to make a *noise*, a *squeak* or a *sound*. **SHHHHH!** Then on the *seventh* day they were to walk around the city *seven* times and on the seventh time they were to blow trumpets LOUDLY and SHOUT praises to God.

And that was it!

God told them that He would do the rest.

So the army set out, making no noise apart from the marching of feet...

Left, right, left, right, left.

The next day they did the same...

Left, right, left, right, left.

And the next, and the next, and the next, and the next until six times they'd walked around the city. *Left, right, left, right, left.*

On the *seventh* day they did exactly the same thing but on the *seventh* time around, when Joshua gave the cue, they blew their trumpets LONG and LOUD.

Toot, toot, toot!

Toot, toot, toot!

Toot, toot, *toot!*

And then the people started to SHOUT. They shouted for freedom, they shouted in victory, they shouted the praises of their God. And then…

CREAK

CRACK

TUMBLE

SMACK

The walls of the great city fell down with a…

SPLAT!

God had gone before them and was giving them a land to call **home.**

Have a think

God had got a big job for Joshua to do, but the job wasn't too big for God! As the people praised God and focused on Him, they saw that God could do anything.

Have a go

Roll up a piece of paper into a cone and stick it together. Then blow down the cone making the sound of a trumpet. Imagine you are one of Israelites blowing the trumpets and shouting praises to God before the walls of Jericho came down.

Have a pray

Dear God, Thank you that you are with me and that nothing I face is too big for you. Amen.

Ruth the Faithful Friend

Ruth 1:1-4:22

After the time of Joshua many seasons came and went. Sometimes the people listened to God and sometimes they didn't, but God always sent leaders to help them find the way back to Him. And God promised that one day THE RESCUER would come.

One year a terrible *famine* struck the land, so Naomi and her family went to *Moab* where there was still food to eat. While they were there, Naomi's husband and two sons *died.*

The sons had married women from Moab and now Naomi and her daughters-in-law, Orpah and Ruth, were all alone. Their hearts and lives were **broken.**

It was then that Naomi decided to go back to her *homeland.*

Naomi said to Orpah and Ruth, "It is better for you to stay with your

own people where you will be looked after." Orpah agreed and *stayed* in Moab. But *Ruth* said, "No. Where *you* go, *I* will go and where *you* stay *I* will stay. *Your* people will become *my* people and *your God* will become *my God*."

Ruth's *heart was set.* So, the two women headed to Israel.

Ruth didn't know anyone there but she was determined to be a **faithful friend** to Naomi so she went to work in a field where she started to gather grain. But when she got there everyone STOPPED and STARED at "**Ruth the Moabite**". She looked **different,** her traditions were **different** and she **didn't belong.**

She had never felt more alone.

But God was *looking after* Ruth and Naomi and it *just so happened* that Ruth had ended up working in the field of a man called Boaz. Boaz was Naomi's relative and he had a *kind* heart. Boaz said to Ruth, "You are *safe* in my field. I have heard how you have looked after Naomi and now may MY GOD under whose wings *you* have come to find *shelter*, look after you."

As the weeks went by Naomi wondered if Boaz would give Ruth a *home* and she came up with a plan. Ruth needed to be *brave* but she did what Naomi said. She crept to Boaz's field in the night, SHHH! Then she fell asleep near to where Boaz was snoring, ZZZZ! Boaz woke up and found her there, which gave him quite a fright, AGHHH! But Ruth said, "Boaz, it's me, Ruth. You are my relative. *Please* will you *shelter* me?"

Ruth was asking Boaz if *he* would **marry her!**

Boaz **wanted** to marry Ruth and he **wanted** to give her and Naomi a home, but he also **wanted** to make sure everything was done in the *right way*.

So, when everything was set in place, **"Boaz the Israelite"** married **"Ruth the Moabite"** and then they had a beautiful *baby boy* called Obed.

Little did anyone know that it was from this new family line that THE RESCUER would eventually come.

Naomi and Ruth *bubbled with happiness*. Their hearts and lives were **starting to mend** and they thanked God for how He was *looking after* them.

Have a think

God is kind and welcomes the foreigner. God was close to Ruth and Naomi in their sadness and also started to bring them new hope. Obed became the father of Jesse who became the father of King David. It was from King David's descendants that THE RESCUER would come!

Have a go

Do you know anyone who has recently come from a different country? Maybe you and your grown-up could do something kind for them.

Have a pray

Dear God, Thank you that you are kind and you are close to us when we are sad or feel like we don't belong. You always have a place in your heart for each of us. Amen.

Hannah and Samuel

1 Samuel 1:1-2:11, 3:1-21, 8:1-10:27, 13:1-14

Once there was a woman called Hannah. Hannah *trusted* God and was God's *friend*. But Hannah didn't have any children and that made her *sad*. What made things worse was that her husband's other wife used to *make fun* of her by chanting, "Ha ha, look at me, I have *lots* of babies and you have NONE! Ha ha ha!" It was *really* **mean!**

Every year Hannah's family would go up to the special place of worship but Hannah's heart felt as *heavy* as can be as she kept on asking God for a little baby.

One year Hannah wasn't smiling, wasn't eating, wasn't doing anything apart from **crying** *big salty tears*, PLOP, PLOP, PLOP. She prayed over and over. "Oh God please hear my *prayer*. Please let me have a baby for I know you *care* about me. If you let me have a little one I'll bring them here so they can grow up *close to you* year after year. *I promise.*"

The priest at the place of worship saw Hannah and said, "*Take heart*, dry those eyes! You're going to have what you asked for, for God has heard your *cries.*"

And sure enough, soon Hannah felt a little *flutter* and *kick* in her tummy. Then there was a stronger *flutter* and *kick*, and then a really strong *flutter* and **kick**. A baby was growing and Hannah was going to be a *Mummy*! Then, WAH, WAH, WAH, Hannah had a *baby boy.* She called the baby **Samuel** and her heart was filled with *joy.*

What a gift!

But Hannah *remembered* her promise to God. So, when Samuel was old enough, Hannah took him back to the special worship place. There, Samuel helped the priest and grew up knowing *God's nearness* and *grace.*

David the Shepherd Lad

1 Samuel 16:1-13

David was a *shepherd lad,* which meant he looked after lots of sheep, *BAAA!*

Every day David would talk to the sheep, care for the sheep, and even keep the sheep safe from GRRRROWLING bears and ROARING lions!

David was *kind,* David was *brave,* David liked to play music and *sing songs* to God. "La laa laaa," sang David. "BA BAA BAAA," replied the sheep.

At night, while a sky full of stars *twinkled* bright, David knew that even though he was just a boy, God who made all those stars was **with him.**

One day God's messenger *Samuel* came to town. Samuel was on a *special mission* to choose the *new king* and God sent him to David's house. David's dad, Jesse, got all of David's older brothers to stand in

front of Samuel. Everyone held their breath as they waited to see what would happen next...

First Samuel looked at Eliab. He was *tall* and *good-looking* and Samuel thought he must be the one. "Yes?" asked Samuel. But God said, "No!" For God wasn't looking at the *outside* of a person, God was looking *into* each person's *heart.* Next came another son, then another and another until *seven sons* had been seen and there were *no other* sons left. But God had *not chosen* any of those! Samuel asked David's dad, "Are there any more sons...*any* at all?" He was told there was only the *youngest,*

David and Goliath

1 Samuel 17:1-58

The Philistines had gone to *war* with the Israelites. The Philistines were meanies and wanted to take over everything.

Every day the Israelite and the Philistine armies stood on opposite hills and shouted at each other, "ARHHHHH". Then the Philistines would bring out their *super weapon*.

He was **BIG.** He was **BOLD.** He was the GIANT GOLIATH!

When the Israelites saw him their knees *KNOCKED* and their tummies *TREMBLED*. Then Goliath would shout, "COME AND FIGHT ME! If you beat me, you will rule over us. But if I beat you, we will rule over you. Send someone to fight… if you dare, HA HA HA!"

But no one dared to fight the giant and so every day the same thing happened, *again and again and again.*

One morning David was taking some yummy cheese to his hungry brothers who were in the Israelite army. He arrived at the exact time Goliath was BOOMING his challenge across the valley. The Israelite army's knees KNOCKED and their tummies TREMBLED, but David said, "**I'll go** and fight this Goliath! Who is *he* to stand in the way of God's people!"

WHAT? David fight Goliath! David was only a shepherd boy and Goliath was ***huge, hairy and horrible!***

But David was determined.

King Saul warned David, "You're not a soldier, you're just a *boy* and Goliath has been fighting since he was a *boy.*" But David told Saul, "I've been looking after my Dad's sheep. When a *GRRROWLING* bear or a ROARING lion came to harm any of them, I would go after them to *protect* the sheep. God who has *kept me safe* from the bear and the lion will *keep me safe* from this Goliath. I know that GOD IS WITH ME."

So David set out to face Goliath taking only his *stick-sling* and *five smooth stones.*

As David stepped onto the battlefield the Israelites *gasped* and the Philistines *jeered.* Goliath took one look at the boy holding his sling and **ROARED,** "Am I a dog that you come against me with a stick?" But David ran straight towards the giant shouting, "You come

*So DAVID set out to face GOLIATH
taking only his STICK-SLING and
FIVE SMOOTH STONES.*

against me with your sword and spear, but I come against you in the name of the Lord and the LORD will rescue us today."

With that David put a *smooth stone* in his sling. He WHIZZED it around his head. He FLUNG it hard into the sky. It ZOOMED through the air. And WHAM hit Goliath right between the eyes.

Goliath *BLINKED*, *WOBBLED,* and then *FELL* to the ground with a giant THUD!

The Israelites cheered and the Philistines ran away.

Hooray, hooray, David had won the day!

God had **rescued** his people with the help of a young shepherd lad called David.

Later on David became king, just like Samuel had said he would, and he was the best king Israel ever had.

Have a think

God was with David and even though others thought he was too young, God used him to do great things.

Have a go

Build a tower of blocks or paper cups with your grown-up. How high can you build it? Now throw a small ball at the tower and watch it topple! Small things can make a big difference!

What small things can you do that could make a big difference to someone else's life?

Have a pray

Dear God, Thank you that you are always with me. Thank you that you can use me to do great things. Please show me how I can make a difference. Amen.

God's Messenger Elijah

1 Kings 17:1-24

Long after Samuel's time, a man called *Elijah* was God's *special messenger*. But *evil* King Ahab was ruler in Israel and he had turned everyone *against* God. Elijah tried to help them find their way back to God, but many people *didn't want to know*.

Once, Elijah *warned* Ahab that there was going to be a *famine* in the land until he said otherwise. And that is what happened. There wasn't a SLITHER, a SCRAPE, or a SCRAP of food anywhere and Ahab was **angry** with Elijah!

So God **hid** Elijah and *looked after him*. Elijah stayed by a little brook that DRIP, DRIP, DRIPPED water and God made ravens SWEEP and SWOOP food to Elijah every day. CAW, CAW, CAW. What a lot of lovely food! Until the brook ran DRIP, DRIP, DRY.

chariot pulled by his *grandest* horses, he CLIP CLOPPED his way to Israel.

CLIP, CLOP, don't stop, CLIP, CLOP, NEIGH!

First he went to see the king but the king couldn't help, so he CLIP CLOPPED to Elisha's house.

CLIP, CLOP, don't stop, CLIP, CLOP, NEIGH!

When he arrived, his horses shook their *splendid* manes and everyone *gazed* at this important man. But Elisha didn't even open the door to him. Instead, he sent his servant with the message, "Go and wash yourself seven times in the Jordan river and then God will heal your skin."

That was NOT what powerful Naaman wanted to hear and he huffed, "He could have at least come out, waved his hand over me and used magic! I will not wash in these MUDDY waters!" And he CLIP CLOPPED angrily away.

But his servants said, "If the messenger had asked you to do something spectacular, would you not have done it?" Naaman knew they were right so he decided to do what Elisha had said.

He went to the muddy waters of the Jordan and…

SPLASH, SPLASH, SPLASH, SPLASH, SPLASH, SPLASH, SPLASH!

Seven times he dipped himself into the river.

When he came out of the water his skin was clean. He had been healed!

Naaman gasped, "Now I know that there is *no other god* in all the world except the Lord your God and from now on I will *trust* and *worship* only Him."

Naaman offered Elisha the *stacks of silver* and *mountains of gold* but Elisha said, "No." *God* had healed Naaman and the thanks and praise belong to *God alone*.

Have a think

Naaman loved doing spectacular things and thought he should be healed in a grand way. But God just wanted him to listen to His words and do what He said, no matter how ordinary it seemed. When he did that, he was healed.

Have a go

Paint a picture of Naaman in his finest clothes dipping in the muddy river!

Have a pray

Dear God, Thank you that you are not looking for spectacular acts, or for what we often think of as important, but you are looking for hearts that simply trust you. Help me simply trust and follow you. Amen.

The Story of Jonah

Jonah 1:1–4:11

One day God said to his friend Jonah, "Go to Nineveh and tell the people that I am sad about the bad things they are doing. If they don't change, disaster will come!

God said, "Jonah, my friend, will you go?" And Jonah said… "NO!"

Jonah quickly packed his bag, ran far away and jumped on a boat heading to Tarshish.

But no matter how far Jonah went, he could never run away from God!

God sent a wild wind over the calm blue sea, stirring up a storm that HOWLED and YOWLED. The waves of the sea went CRASH and the floor of Jonah's boat went CREAK. The storm was so HUGE that the sailors yelled, "EEEKK! We're going to die. What has caused these MASSIVE waves?"

Jonah sighed, "It's my fault. I'm running away from the God who made the sea! The only way to stop the *HOWL* is to throw me overboard, otherwise you all will drown!"

And so with a HEAVE and a S P L A S H the sailors threw Jonah into the stormy waves. In a blink, the sea stilled and all the sailors were saved. PHEW!

....

But what about Jonah?

Down, down, deep down down, Jonah sank into the heart of the sea. Afraid and alone he cried out, "My God, please rescue me!"

God was still with Jonah and was still his friend. So, God sent ONE **BIG** FISH with a tail that *SWISHED* and a mouth that opened really W I D E . And in one big GULP, Jonah was swallowed alive!

For three long days Jonah sat in the smelly belly of the giant fish and there, Jonah had some time to think. "Um… dear God," said Jonah with a sniff, "I'm sorry. Thank you for helping me. Thank you that you still love me. You really are the Great Rescuer."

Then the big fish did a giant **BURP** and *SPAT* Jonah out and onto dry land. And God asked him again, "Will you tell the people of Nineveh I want to help them out of their mess?" And Jonah said… "Yes!"

So, God sent ONE **BIG** FISH with a tail that swished and a mouth that opened really **WIDE**. And in one big GULP, Jonah was swallowed alive!

……………

When the people of Nineveh heard God's message, they said sorry to God. God heard their prayer and gave them a fresh start, right then and there.

But Jonah moaned, "God, I knew you would show them kindness because you love people so much. I didn't want them rescued, I wanted them to pay for the wrong they have done!" And he sat down in the hot, hot sun with a **"HUFF!"**

God made a green plant grow up fast to give Jonah some leafy shade. Jonah said, "Ahh, a plant to help me today." But then a wiggly worm munched through the plant until it wilted away. Now Jonah was even more cross and shouted **"AGHHHHH,** God I've had **ENOUGH!"**

But God said, "Jonah, my friend. You care about this plant even though you didn't make it or cause it to grow. How much more do I care about this great city of Nineveh with thousands of people in it? People who I love and people who I know?"

Have a think

God loves us all very much and is our Great Rescuer. In the story of Jonah, who do you think God rescues?

Have a go

Make a den out of sheets and pretend you are in the belly of a big fish. What do you think it would look like? What do you think it would smell like? What do you think Jonah felt like when he was in the fish and when he was back on the dry land?

Have a pray

Dear God, Thank you that you always love me and give me the chance to start again, no matter what has happened. Thank you that you are my Rescuer. Amen.

The Fiery Flames

Daniel 1:1-8, 3:1-30

Once there were four friends called Daniel, Hananiah, Mishael and Azariah and they had all been taken captive by the Babylonians. This meant they were *forced* to live in Babylon and serve the Babylonian king. In Babylon the people *worshipped* lots of different gods. But the four were *friends of God* and they wanted to **stay true** to Him.

In Babylon they were given the names Belteshazzar, Shadrach, Meshach and Abednego, but they *never* forgot who they really were and the God they loved.

....

This is what happened to Shadrach, Meshach and Abednego...

The Fiery Flames

One year the king of Babylon made a huge *golden statue* and said, "When you hear the TOOT, TOOT of the flute and the PIP, PIP of the pipe and the HONK, HONK of the horn, everyone MUST fall flat on their face and *worship* this golden god that I have made. If you do not, you will be thrown into HOT, HOT, FIERY FLAMES!"

So when everyone heard the TOOT, TOOT, *PIP, PIP* and HONK, HONK they fell down on their faces and *worshipped* the statue. But Shadrach, Meshach and Abednego *didn't.*

The king told them, "You need to bow before the statue or I'll throw you in the *fire* and *no god* will be able to rescue you from that!"

Shadrach, Meshach and Abednego said, "Our God is **very able to rescue us** from the flames, but **even if He does not**, we **WILL NOT** serve your gods or *worship* the statue."

The king was angry and ordered, "Throw Shadrach, Meshach and Abednego into the HOT, HOT, FIERY FLAMES!" The flames S I Z Z L E D and *SPARKED* as the three men were tied up and thrown into the fire. OH NO!

But after a while the king gasped, "What's happening? I can see *four men* walking in the flames and the forth looks like a *son of the gods.* Their God has RESCUED them!"

Shadrach, Meshach and Abednego *walked out* of the fiery flames. They were *not hurt,* they were *not burned* and they *did not even smell of smoke!*

The king shouted, "TOOT, TOOT, *PIP, PIP* and HONK, HONK to the God of Shadrach, Meshach and Abednego who has sent his *angel* to RESCUE them. They *trusted* in Him and were *willing* to give up their *own lives* instead of worshipping any other god!"

God was **with** his friends Shadrach, Meshach and Abednego in the fire and He RESCUED them from those HOT, HOT, FIERY FLAMES! TOOT, TOOT, *PIP, PIP* **HONK, HONK!**

Have a think

The friends trusted God so much that even if He didn't rescue them, they would not worship any other god. Sometimes in life we see God's dramatic rescue like they did, at other times God walks with us through hard situations and rescues us in a different way.

Either way, God has promised He is always with us.

Have a go

The friends were very brave to choose not to bow to the statue when everyone else did. Tell your grown-up about a time where you have had to make a brave choice. Ask your grown-up to tell you about a time they had to make a brave choice.

Have a pray

Thank you, God, that you are able to rescue us. Thank you that sometimes you rescue us dramatically and sometimes you walk through the hard situations with us. Thank you that whatever is happening, you are always with us. Amen.

Daniel and the Lions' Den

Daniel 6:1-28

This is what happened to Daniel when Darius was king of Babylon...

Daniel was *very wise* and King Darius made him a *very important* advisor in his kingdom. This made the other advisers **VERY JEALOUS** and they wanted him out of the way. But Daniel was *honest* and they couldn't trip him up over *anything* he did. So, they thought LONG and HARD until they came up with a *sneaky* plan.

Daniel prayed to God *three times every day* and *everyone* knew that his heart was *true* to the God he loved. So, the *sly* advisers said to the king, "Oh, our *super-duper excellency* you are the best king ever. We think *everyone* should only PRAY TO YOU and if they don't they should be *thrown to the lions*."

The king was a teeny bit vain and said, "What a great idea, everyone must pray to me or they will be *lion lunch*. Hooray!"

The advisers giggled with glee saying, "Daniel will NOT stop praying to his God for anyone. We've set a *super-duper* trap!"

And they were right! Daniel would NOT stop praying to his God even if it meant his own life was in danger. So, three times a day he sat by his window and *carried on* praying to God.

The advisers smirked, "Tee hee, we've got Daniel now." And they ran back to the king saying, "Oh our *super-duper* king! You said that everyone should pray to you and if they didn't they'd be thrown to the lions. Well, **Daniel is still praying to his God** so that means…he has to be LION DINNER, hee hee!"

Darius was sad because he liked Daniel, but he couldn't go back on his word. So he quietly said, "Throw Daniel to the lions!"

The lions were FIERCE and FEISTY, they were TETCHY and TOOTHY and most of all they were HUNGRY! With *gnashing jaws* and *sharpened claws* they waited for their dinner as **Daniel was thrown into THE DEN OF DEATH.** Oh No!

That night King Darius couldn't sleep a wink and early in the morning he rushed to the lions' den calling out, "Daniel, did your God *rescue* you from the lions' teeth?"

Daniel yawned and sleepily said, "Morning, King Darius. Yes, my

"Have you got a room?" Joseph asked at one inn, and then "PLEASE, we need a space, any place?" at another. But the answer came back over and over, time and time again, "NO!", "NO!", "NO!"

"OOO! Look at that star!" one of them gasped. "AHH! It means a great king has been born!" another said.

HOORAY!

The wise travellers got off their camels, got down on their knees and *bowed* before baby Jesus.

They gave him gifts of gold, frankincense and myrrh. Gifts fit for a KING.

The wise men had travelled a long way, but it was worth every single sandy step because God's RESCUER was for everyone. And our three wise men actually got to meet him!

Have a think

God wanted everyone to know about Jesus, whether they lived nearby like the shepherds, or were foreigners from far away like the three wise men.

Have a go

Paint some more cardboard tubes; one for each of the wise men, then put them next to baby Jesus too!

Have a pray

Dear Jesus, Thank you that you are God's special gift to everyone in the whole world. Amen.

A Dunk in the River

Matthew 3:1-17

Years had passed, Jesus was now all *grown up* and it was time for **God's great rescue plan** to really start.

The first thing that needed to happen was a DUNK in the river. So Jesus went to see his cousin John, whose mum was Elizabeth.

John had been telling everyone, "Get ready, get ready, GET READY! THE RESCUER is coming. God **loves us** and wants us to be able to be his friends. It's time to say sorry to God and start again!"

John would then DUNK people under the water with a SPLISH, and they would come out of the water with a SPLASH.

It was called being *baptised* and it was a bit like having a bath! It showed that the people wanted to be *washed clean* from things they had done that had messed up their friendship with God.

When Jesus arrived at the river he said, "Hello, John. I want to be baptised today!"

But John said, **"No no no no no no NO!**

"YOU don't need to be baptised! You're already God's friend and your life is clean through and through. It's me who should be baptised by you. You are THE RESCUER."

But Jesus said, "I want to be baptised to show everyone the way. It is the right thing to do." So John said, "OK!"

Jesus put his toes into the cold river, BRR! Soon he was up to his ankles, BRRRR and then his waist, BRRRRRR!

John DUNKED him under the water with a SPLISH and he came out of the water with a SPLASH.

Suddenly, a BRIGHT LIGHT BLAZED from the sky! The clouds OPENED WIDE and God's *Holy Spirit* settled on Jesus like a *peaceful* dove. Then everyone could hear God from heaven saying, "This is MY Son who I really love and I'm very happy with him."

WOW!

What a start!

God wanted EVERYONE to know that Jesus was his special Son. Jesus' work had now begun.

Jesus said, "I want to be BAPTISED to show everyone the way. It is the RIGHT thing to do."

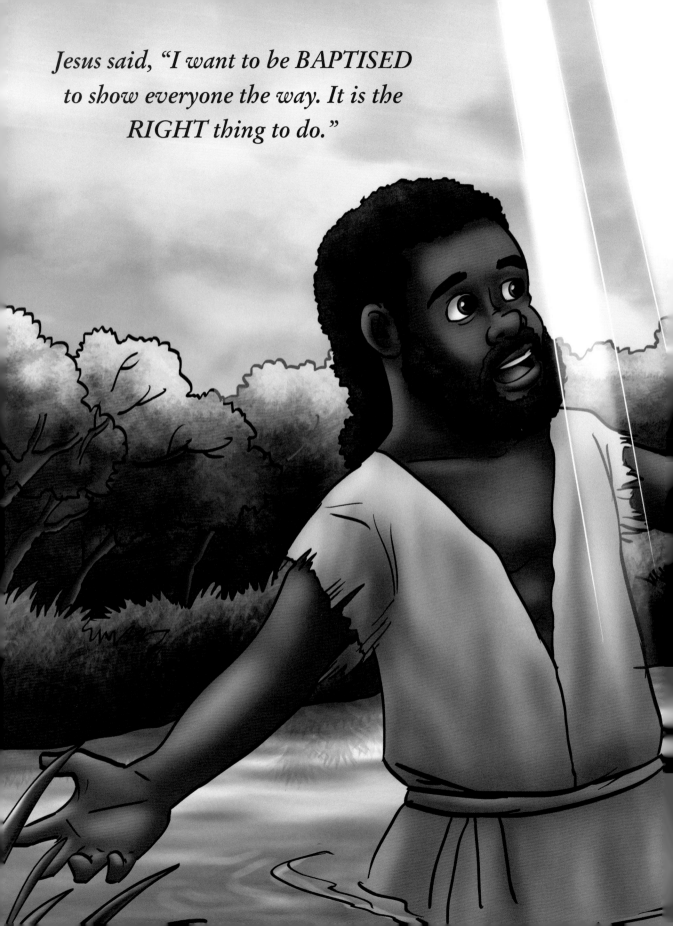

Jesus was alone and had no food
for forty days *and* forty nights.

The deceiver then took Jesus to a very high place and smirked, "If you really are God's *much loved* Son, then jump off this high spot and God will catch you!" But Jesus said, "No. It is written, 'Don't try to make God prove who he is.'"

Then the slithery one said, "If you bow down and worship me, I'll give you all the fame, success and power you could ever want!" But Jesus said, "Get away from me. I will worship only God."

And with that the sneaky deceiver left Jesus alone.

Jesus had *passed* a **BIG test.**

He did not fall for the devil's tricks. HE was strong enough to say **NO.** And so, where Adam and Eve had made bad choices in that garden long ago, Jesus *made good choices* and trusted in his Father.

Have a think

In life we have small and big choices to make. Jesus wants to help us trust in God and not to fall for harmful tricks. Jesus is with us, he can help us say no to bad choices just like he did.

Have a go

Talk with your grown-up about a small or big choice you have to make. Now, talk about what a bad choice would look like and what a good choice would look like.

Have a pray

Dear Jesus, Please help me trust you more and more. Help me say no to bad choices and yes to you. Amen.

Twelve Special Friends

Matthew 4:18-22

One day Jesus was walking by the *Sea of Galilee.* The green-grey waves *lapped* the pebbly beach and Jesus made his way over the stony shore with a CRUNCH, CRUNCH, CRUNCH. Just then, he saw two brothers, Simon and Andrew, they were fishermen and they were **busy**! They had a big net on their boat and would throw it into the water with a WHOOSH...SPLASH and then pull it out of the water with a HEAVE...SPLOSH. When the big net landed back in the boat, it would be full of *wriggly fish...*SPLISH.

Jesus called out to the brothers, "Hey, let's be friends! Come and spend time with me and learn all about God and his great love. Follow me and I'll teach *you* to fish for people."

The brothers had *always* just been ordinary fishermen and they were *surprised* that Jesus wanted *them* to be *his* friends. Straight away, they threw down their nets with a **THUD...PLONK** and smiled, "We'd love to be your friends, we'll follow you!"

Jesus also spotted two other fishermen brothers called James and John and he picked them to be in his group. Later on he chose some more people until he had **twelve special friends.** Twelve friends who were now part of **God's great rescue plan.**

They loved spending time with Jesus, listening to him tell his stories and learning from him all about Father God.

Soon, they would start to help others get to know God too.

Have a think

Jesus' friends were called his "disciples" and they were especially picked by Jesus. Jesus thinks you are special and he wants to be friends with you.

Have a go

Draw lots of fish on a big piece of paper, decorate them and cut them out. Write your name and the names of your family or friends on the back of different fish. Put all the fish on the floor and make sure you can't see any of the names! Now, pretend to go fishing. Can you pick out the fish with your name on it? Can you pick out the fish with your friends' name on it?

Have a pray

Dear Jesus, Thank you that you love me. Thank you that you have picked me and want *me* to be your friend. I want to spend time with you and get to know you more. Amen.

Wise Words

Matthew 5:43-48, 6:5-15, 22:35-40

Jesus enjoyed teaching people about his *Father God,* about how to live close to Him, about **how much** God LOVES every single one of us. The people would *gather* around and Jesus would help them *understand* many things.

One time someone asked Jesus what the most important law in life was and Jesus said, **"Love, love, love.** *Love God and love people.* It's as *simple* as that."

Another time he told them, "*Love* the people you think of as your enemies and *pray* for those who do wrong to you. Because *God is kind* and *loves us soooooooooo* much with that sort of *giving love.*"

Jesus also taught the people how to *pray.* He told them, "Prayer is about talking to God. You *don't need* to use big language. You *don't need* to show off. Just speak to God like you would a *friend.* He will

listen to you and you can listen to Him."

And then Jesus taught them a good prayer that they could *all* pray…

"Our loving Father who is in heaven,

May your wonderful name be celebrated, oh yes!

May your good kingdom come,

And may your plans and purposes be done

On earth, just like they are done in heaven.

Please give us everything we need

For each and every day,

Please forgive us for the things we have done wrong,

As we choose to forgive those who have done wrong to us.

Keep us away from bad choices,

And rescue us from every evil scheme.

For the power, glory and absolute splendour are all yours

Now, forever and always."

And all the people nodded their heads and said, "We agree, **Amen.**"

Have a think

God loves us so much that he sent the gift of His special Son Jesus. We can love others, because God first loved us. Is there anyone you could show love to?

Have a go

Spend some time praying to Jesus. You can tell him how you feel. You can tell him what is going on in your life. Why not listen to see what he might say back to you.

Have a pray

Dear Jesus, Thank you that you love me. Thank you that you show me how to love God and love people. Please help me do both. Amen.

The Woman at the Well

John 4:1-30

The Jewish people stayed away *from an area called* Samaria. *They absolutely DID NOT like the Samaritan people! Jesus was Jewish but Jesus was* different.

One day Jesus walked STRAIGHT *into* **Samaria** and stopped by a well. It was HOT and Jesus was **thirsty**. Just then a woman came to get water from the well.

Most women were at the well when it was the *cool* part of the day. They would go with their friends, they would CHAT, CHAT, CHAT, they would collect water from the well and enjoy a cool drink, SPLISH, SPLASH, AHHHHHH!

But NO ONE wanted to be at the well with *this* woman, so she went *on her own when it was* HOT, HOT, HOT.

Jesus saw the woman and said, "Hello, please will you give me a drink of water?"

The woman was SHOCKED. Jesus was a *Jew* and Jesus was a *man*! Jewish men *never, ever, **ever*** spoke to Samaritan women! She said, "How can *you* ask *me* for a drink?"

Jesus smiled and said, "If you knew how *kind and loving* God is and *who I am*, you would ask me and I would *give you fresh, clean, **living water***.

The woman asked, "*How?* You don't have a jug, *where* would you get this *water*?" Jesus said, "When you drink well-water you get thirsty again. But the spirit-life I give is like *crystal clear water, bubbling* up on the inside of a person for *now* and *for eternity*. It's like COLD water on a HOT day that refreshes your soul. AHHHHHH!"

In her heart the woman felt parched and she said, "Please give me this type of water!"

Jesus looked at her with love and began to talk with her about the story of her life. The woman was embarrassed because she knew her life was in a bit of a *mess*. That was why NO ONE wanted to be at the well with her.

She said, "I can see you are from God and know things *only* He could know. When THE RESCUER comes he will explain *everything* and help us be *close to God*!"

Jesus looked at the woman and said, "*I am* THE RESCUER!"

Just then Jesus' twelve friends came over to the well and were SHOCKED to find him talking to a *Samaritan woman*. But the woman joyfully ran into town saying, "Come and meet Jesus. HE told me everything I've *ever* done. Could he be THE RESCUER?"

Now, the *people* were all SHOCKED and wondered what had happened to *this* woman. So they rushed out to meet Jesus for *themselves.*

Have a think

No one wanted to talk with this woman, but Jesus welcomed her, loved her and wanted her to have the new life, the living water, that only He can give.

Have a go

Have a drink of cold water. Imagine how nice it is to drink cold water on a hot day.

Have a pray

Dear Jesus, Thank you that everyone is welcome with you no matter what their life story has been. Thank you that you want to give me your life-giving water that bubbles up in my soul now and for eternity. Amen.

The Wise and Silly Builder

Matthew 7:24-29

Everyone wanted to hear what Jesus had to say because he really *knew God and was helping them get to know Him too*. One day Jesus smiled and said, "The people who listen to my words and then *put them into practice*, what are they like?" The crowd were quiet, they were ready for a story!

"Well…" said Jesus, "they are like a *very wise* man who wanted to build a house. And being *very, very wise* he decided to build his house on *solid rock*.

"So he built his house with a TAP, TAP, TAP and a WHACK, WHACK, WHACK. He made a window and he made a door, he put on a roof and he laid a floor with a TAP, TAP, TAP and a WHACK, WHACK, WHACK. Until the house was finished. HOORAY! But then it started to rain and rain! It PELTED and POUNDED

and GUSHED some more, against the windows and the door. It HIT the roof and PUMMELLED the wall but the **rock was strong** and the house **didn't fall.**

"And what about the people who hear my words and then *don't do anything* about them, what are they like?" asked Jesus. The crowd leaned a bit closer as Jesus said…

"Well, they are like *a very silly* man who also wanted to build a house. And being *very, very silly,* he thought he'd build his house on *soft wet sand.*

So he built his house with a TAP, TAP, TAP and a WHACK, WHACK, WHACK. He made a window and he made a door, he put on a roof and he laid a floor with a TAP, TAP, TAP and a WHACK, WHACK, WHACK. Until the house was finished. HOORAY!

But then it started to rain and rain! It PELTED and POUNDED and GUSHED some more, against the windows and the door. It HIT the roof and PUMMELLED the wall but the *sand wasn't strong* and the house started to…

Tipple,

Topple,

Wibble,

Wobble,

Slip,

Slide

and

F

a

l

l!"

Have a think

Jesus' words are like solid rock. They give us a strong foundation to build our lives on. And when we do that, we're like the wise man in this story!

Have a go

The next time you are at a beach or sand pit, build a sandcastle on the soft sand. Test how easy it is to knock it over!

Have a pray

Dear Jesus, Please help me build my life on who you are and on your words, for they are like solid rock. Amen.

The Man on a Mat

Mark 2:1-12

Everywhere Jesus went *crowds* of people followed. They wanted to hear his words and they wanted to see him make the sick people well. Because, *everywhere* Jesus went, he *healed* people!

One day Jesus was in a house that was *packed* with a crowd. There was *no room* to *skip* or *jump* and barely room to *breathe.* There was definitely *no room* to get through the door to see Jesus. So, four friends thought they would use the *roof* instead! Great idea!

Suddenly the sound of C R R R , CRRR, C R R R could be heard as the four friends made a *small hole* in the roof. C R R R , CRRR, C R R R they chipped away until it became a *bigger hole* and then, C R R R , CRRR, C R R R it became a *massive hole*!

One of the friends looked through the gap and beamed, "This is the right place, let's get him down!" Then, they carefully *lowered* a *man on a mat* through the *massive hole* until he was *right in front of Jesus.*

The man was lying on the mat because he *couldn't walk.* But, his friends **knew** that if they *just* got him to Jesus, *Jesus would heal him.*

Jesus smiled at the **brave, confident trust** of the four friends. And he smiled with love at the man on the mat saying, "The things you've done wrong in the past are forgiven, *you can be friends with God.*"

Some of the religious leaders were cross and thought to themselves, "Who is this Jesus? *Only* God can forgive and make a person's heart clean."

Jesus knew what they were thinking and so he said, "Is it easier to forgive or to heal? But just so you know the power of God is at work in me to do *both,* I will heal the man on the mat too." Then looking at the man on the mat Jesus said, "Get up *friend,* pick up your mat and go home!" And…

He did!

Hooray!

The man *stood up* on *legs that were now strong!* He scooped up his mat and with a *skip* and a *jump* he pushed his way out of the crowded house and *danced all the way home!*

Have a think

Jesus loved the confident trust of the four friends. It was their faith that made the way for a miracle. Jesus also loved making the man on the mat well and giving him a fresh start.

Have a go

Do you know someone who would love to know Jesus' healing or friendship? Why not spend a bit of time praying for them and asking Jesus to do something in their life, just like he did with the man on the mat.

Have a pray

Dear Jesus, Thank you that you are the healer and you love to give us a fresh start so that we can be friends with God. Amen.

A Big Storm

Mark 4:35-41

One day Jesus and his friends were in a boat on the lake called the Sea of Galilee. The sun was out, the sky was blue, and Jesus fell asleep as the waves *gently rocked the boat* with a SWISH, SWISH, SWISH.

When suddenly **huge dark clouds** rolled across the sky, the wind WHISTLED and the waves grew **wild** with a SWISH, SWISH, SWISH.

The thunder CRACKED and the rain POUNDED down and everyone in the boat thought they would drown as the waves went SWISH, SWISH, SWISH.

But Jesus was fast asleep, peaceful as can be. Until his friends woke him up and shouted, "We're going to die, rescue us from the sea!"

Jesus looked at his friends and said, "Why is your faith still *so* small.

Jesus was fast asleep,
peaceful as can be.

Don't you know that God is **King** over all!" And with that Jesus lifted up his hands, lifted up his gaze, and then he simply *spoke* to the waves, "Peace, be still. Shhhhh, quieten down."

And suddenly the waves **stopped** and the w i n d

didn't

make

a sound.

The sun came out and the sky turned blue and the friends in the boat gasped at what they now knew. They said, "Jesus holds the very power of God! Even the wind and the waves do whatever he says. Maybe he **is** THE RESCUER who has come to save the day!"

And the waves gently rocked the boat with a S W I S H , S W I S H , S W I S H .

Have a think

Jesus is powerful and can do anything. When life feels like a storm, he can bring peace and calm for he is always with you.

Have a go

When it is bath time pretend that one of your bath toys is the boat on the lake. Can you make the water splash like a storm? Then, watch as the water settles to calm again.

Have a pray

Thank you, God, that you are **King** over all. You can do anything! Please help me know that you are with me even when things seem like a giant storm. You can make things peaceful again and I trust you to rescue me. Amen.

Brand New Life

Mark 5:21-43

When Jesus got back from the other side of the lake a huge crowd gathered around him. Just then, one of the religious leaders called Jairus *pushed* through the people and *fell* at Jesus feet. He gasped, "Good teacher, *please* come quickly. My twelve-year-old girl is *dying*. But, if *you* put *your* hands on her, she *will live.*"

So Jesus started walking with Jairus towards his house.

While they were on the way the message came, "Jairus, don't bother Jesus anymore. Your little girl is dead."

When Jesus heard this he shook his head, he looked Jairus in the eye and he simply said, *"Don't be afraid, just believe!"* and Jesus carried on walking towards the house.

When they arrived, everyone was very sad and there was *weeping* and *wailing* as they cried for the girl. But Jesus shook his head, looked them all in the eye and he simply said, "She's just asleep, *she's not dead!*" They laughed because they knew that she had *died.* But Jesus carried on towards the little girl's room.

He took his friends Peter, James and John along with the girl's parents and they all went inside…

to where the girl was lying…

     still.

       No breath.

        No heartbeat.

          No life.

But, Jesus shook his head. He looked at the girl, took her hand and simply said, "Little girl, I say to you, ***wake up from the dead.***"

And in *a* **breath**

    and a **heartbeat,**

       she was *alive!*

Everyone was amazed as the girl giggled and twirled. Jesus had filled her body with **brand new life.**

Have a think

Jesus is the life bringer and Jesus is with us. He can do miracles and bring new life even in the worst of situations.

Have a go

Paint one picture of a happy face and one picture of a sad face. Cut them both out. Retell the story and as you do, hold up the face you think the people in the story would have looked like.

Have a pray

Dear Jesus, Thank you that you are the life bringer. Please breathe your new life into my heart and the situations I'm thinking about right now. Amen.

Hidden Treasure

Matthew 13:44

It was time for another story. Jesus gathered the people close and said, "What is God's kingdom like? Well, it's a bit like…

"A man finding a *box* hidden in a *muddy field*.

"But this was not an ordinary box, *no no no no no!*

"It was a *very special box*, it was a *very precious box*,

"It was a *big box full* of *treasure*.

"The man was so *excited* and *delighted* about the *treasure* that

"He went home,

"He sold *everything* he had,

"And he went back to buy the field.

"Now the *big box* of *special*,

"*precious, treasure,*

"was HIS!"

Have a think

God's gift to us of Jesus is like that box of treasure. Treasure that is worth giving everything for. And when we have Jesus at the centre of our lives, we find that we are the ones who have actually gained the greatest treasure.

Have a go

Fill a shoebox with some special toys. Now, act out this story using your box of treasure!

Have a pray

Dear Jesus, Thank you that your gift of love, forgiveness and peace with God, is worth everything. Amen.

One Small Seed

Mark 4:30-32

Jesus told the people lots of stories to help them understand what God was like and how the things of God's Kingdom worked. And so once again, THE RESCUER*, the King of God's Kingdom began to teach them.*

"Look at the *little* mustard seed," said Jesus. "It's a *tiny, teeny, weeny* seed, one of the *smallest* seeds you've ever seen. BUT

"When this seed is *planted* and begins to *grow*,

"It shoots *up* and *out*,

"Until birds can come and build their nests in its branches.

"What started *so small* now grows *strong* and *tall*,

"and becomes the *most beautiful* tree of all.

"And that is what God's Kingdom is like."

Have a think

Sometimes we can think that the gifts of God within us are very small. Gifts like His love, His peace, His kindness, His joy. But it is those things that can grow full of life and make the world a bit more beautiful, showing others what God is like.

Have a go

With your grown-up's help, plant a little seed in some soil. Watercress or beans are easy to have a go with. Give the seed a bit of water and some sunlight and watch it grow!

Have a pray

Dear Jesus, Please help my life be good soil so that the gifts you give can grow in me and make the world a bit more peaceful, a bit more loving, a bit more beautiful. Amen.

One Great Picnic

John 6:1-15

Jesus had been telling super stories all day long. Now it was late and everyone's tummies were RUMBLY and GRUMBLY! But there wasn't *any* food *anywhere*. Not a *bake*, not a *cake*, not a *slice*, not even a *crumb* for the tiny *mice*! SQUEAK!

Well, there was a *tiny, teeny, weeny* bit of food…a little boy's packed lunch! He had two *bites of fish* and five *bites of bread*!

Yummy!

But what good was one packed lunch when FIVE THOUSAND PEOPLE had RUMBLY, GRUMBLY TUMMIES!

Jesus smiled and said, "I know! Let's feed them *all*!" Jesus' friends began to PANIC! "Ahhhhhhh!" they said. "Where could we get enough food for *all* these people to be well fed?" But, the boy thought

he might be able to help. He knew it wasn't much but if Jesus wanted it, he would give him the *bites of fish* and *bites of bread*.

Jesus did want it. It was just what he needed!

Everyone sat down ready to eat, Jesus thanked his Father God for what they were about to *munch*, and he and his friends gave out the little boy's *packed lunch*.

And the food just kept on *going* and *going* and *going*! It DIDN'T run out. It DIDN'T

stop! The people laughed and their bellies popped!
WOW!
They ALL had *one giant* picnic from a *tiny, teeny, weeny* bit of food. And ALL those RUMBLY, GRUMBLY, TUMMIES were well fed, with those two *bites of fish* and five *bites of bread!*
Yummy, yummy, yummy!

Have a think

God can do amazing things! Sometimes we think that what we have to offer Him is too small. But when we give what we have to Jesus – whether that's something we're good at, something we have, a little bit of faith, a little bit of prayer, a little bit of time – he can do miracles!

Have a go

Why not have a picnic with your toys or your friends. Retell the story as you share out the food!

Have a pray

Dear Jesus, Thank you that you can do anything and you really are amazing!

Water Walking

Matthew 14:22-33

After everyone had gone home, Jesus told his friends, "Go over to the other side of the lake and I'll meet you there later." So, the group set out in their boat and Jesus set off up a mountain. He wanted to have a *quiet space* where he could pray and talk with his Father God.

In the *middle* of the night, the boat was in the *middle* of the lake and, even though they didn't know it yet, the friends were in the *middle of a miracle*. The wind WHOOSHED and the waves PUSHED the boat from *side* to *side*. The friends rowed hard and tried to keep the boat safe, *all through the night*.

Then, with the first glint of morning light, Jesus began to WALK ON THE WATER. He was heading towards the boat. WHAT! How could it be? He stayed *afloat*! He didn't sink, and his friends

Jesus began to WALK ON THE WATER.

Transformed

Matthew 17:1-13

Jesus' twelve friends spent all their time with Jesus. Every minute, every hour, every day. He was their leader and everywhere Jesus went, they went too. They believed in him and knew him very well.

One day Jesus took three of his special friends, Peter, James and John, up a mountain. And when they were at the very top something *remarkable* happened.

Suddenly, there was a BLAZE of BRILLIANT LIGHT and in a BLINK, Jesus was TRANSFORMED.

He wasn't just Jesus the good teacher and good friend anymore, now he was clothed with *pure, shining, glory* from heaven.

Next, Moses and Elijah from a long time ago popped up and stood next to Jesus.

The Little Ones and Jesus

Mark 10:13-16

The religious leaders *didn't like* Jesus very much. They *didn't like* him claiming to be God's Son. They *didn't like* all the *people* following him. But others *loved* being close to Jesus, especially *children*.

They *loved* his *smile* that *twinkled* with *fun,* they *loved* his *stories* that made them *giggle,* they *loved* feeling *safe* with him.

One day, a *gaggle* of children were SKIPPING and HOPPING and JUMPING around Jesus. The mums and dads had brought them to him so he could pray God's goodness over them. Jesus *laughed* as he happily picked the little ones up and started to pray.

But Jesus' twelve friends were in a *huff*. They mumbled, "Jesus is busy. He's THE RESCUER and has *more important* things to be doing than playing with little ones." And they told the parents, "Take these

children away from here, can't you see they're in the way. *Clear off!*"

But Jesus was *very cross* with the friends and said to the children, "It's alright. You are *loved* and *always welcome* with me." And then he told everyone else,

"Let the little ones come close to me, don't *ever* stop them, for God's Kingdom *belongs* to them and those who are like them. Anyone who doesn't welcome God's gift of friendship with the *trust* and *wonder* of a child, will not be able to easily find the way."

And he opened his arms *wide*,

He *scooped* up the little ones,

And gave them *heaven's warmest smile*.

Have a think

Jesus loved the children, they were always welcome with him. Jesus loves you and you are always welcome with him too.

Have a go

Imagine that you are one of those children meeting Jesus. What do you think he looked like? What do you think he sounded like? What do you think it felt like to meet him?

Have a pray

Dear Jesus, Thank you that you love me and I'm always welcome with you. Amen.

Blind Bartimaeus

Mark 10:46-52

One day, a man called Bartimaeus was sitting outside the city of Jericho. He was *blind* and so was begging for money to survive.

Suddenly there was a *commotion*, which was really *loud*. There was lots of excitement and the CHATTER of a *crowd*. They were making *so much noise* that Bartimaeus wondered what it was all about. He heard that Jesus was passing his way and he knew that this could be the very day for him where **everything changed.**

He'd heard about Jesus, he knew his name. Jesus was the man who made the blind eyes *see*, the deaf ears *hear* and the broken heart *set free*. Jesus was the one people said was the THE RESCUER from God who could even raise the dead.

Bartimaeus didn't waste a minute and he *shouted,* **"Jesus!**

Have mercy on me!"

Well, the crowd told him to HUSH! They didn't want this beggar getting in the way, they were in a *rush* to see what Jesus would do next. But Bartimaeus didn't care what they said and so he shouted LONG and he shouted LOUD,

"JESUS!!! JESUS!!! JESUS!!! Rescue me!!!"

Jesus heard, he stopped and he smiled, "Bring the man through this crowd."

The people said to Bartimaeus, "Quick, today could be your day, Jesus is calling for *you to come*!" Bartimaues *jumped* up on his feet and stumbled his way to Jesus right there on the dusty street.

Jesus looked at Bartimaeus and loved him through and through, he said to the blind beggar, "*What* would you like me to do for you?"

"Good teacher," sobbed Bartimaeus, "please, I want to see."

Jesus smiled and said, "Because you *believe*, you will *now have sight.*"

And, PING, Bartimaeus could see *everything* in colours **BOLD and BRIGHT!**

WOW!!!

Now Bartimaeus was *shouting* praise to *God most high,* who had looked on him and had ***heard his cry!***

Have a think

Jesus heard Bartimaeus' cry. He listened, he stopped and he did something to help. Jesus brought light and sight to Bartimaeus' life and everything for Bartimaeus changed.

Have a go

Ask your grown-up to put a blindfold over your eyes. Now try and walk around without bumping into anything. It's quite hard! Next, ask your grown-up to take your blindfold off and walk around again. What a difference light and sight can make!

Have a pray

Dear Jesus, Thank you that you hear my prayers and you can do anything. You can bring light into any dark situation. Amen.

Zacchaeus and the Tree

Luke 19:1-10

By now everyone had heard about Jesus and wondered if he really was THE RESCUER from God sent to set things right and to bring peace. So, wherever Jesus went everyone CROWDED around.

One day, Jesus had gone to the city of Jericho and the streets were BUZZING with people wanting to *see him*, wanting to *touch him*, wanting to be *near him*.

In that city was a man called Zacchaeus and he also wanted to see Jesus.

The people didn't like Zacchaeus because he was a *tax collector*. That meant it was his job to *take* money from the people for the mean Romans who were in charge. But he didn't just take what he *should*, no! Zachhaeus would take *whatever* he *could*. A *bit* here and a *bit* there, a *lot* here and a *lot* there, to fill his *own purse* full of money!

Zacchaeus was also *very short* and so he couldn't see over the TALL crowd.

Zachhaeus *stood on his tiptoes* and then *jumped in the air*, he *hopped from foot to foot* saying, "Please let me through, I want to see Jesus too." But the people *didn't care*. They JOSTLED and RUSHED, SHOVED and PUSHED Zacchaeus right out of the way!

What was Zacchaeus going to do?

Just then he saw a nearby *fig tree* and said to himself, "If I climb those branches I'll be able to see, what a great idea, clever me!"

So Zacchaeus start to climb **up, up, up** the tree. He got a great view just as Jesus was passing by!

THREW his arms around **his boy.**

The tired and *smelly* son started his speech, "Dad, I'm so sorry, I…" But he didn't get any further because his dad hugged him with all his might. The dad put his cloak over the boy's shoulders, gave him shoes and a ring that showed he belonged and said, *"My son, it's alright. I love you, it's time to come home."*

The dad was *so happy* he shouted, "Let's have a party, it's time to celebrate!"

The older son, who had been at his father's house the *whole* time, was cross and *huffed*, "This boy of yours has *wasted* everything and now we're throwing him a party! I *never* have a party!" and he went off on his own. But the dad said, *"Son, I love you very much and all I have is yours. But we had to celebrate because my beloved lost son has now come home."*

Have a think

Father God loves us no matter what. He always has a place for us in his heart. He is always looking for us when we are far away. He always wants to welcome us so we can be close to him.

Have a go

Can you make a play-doh model of the dad hugging his lost son? What do you think the son would have felt like when he realised he was still loved and still welcome?

Have a pray

Dear Father God, Thank you that your arms are always open for me. When I make mistakes and feel far away from you, help me know that you always love me and want to welcome me home. Amen.

The Good Good Shepherd

John 10:11-18

Jesus often used stories and picture words to help people understand who he was. One day Jesus said,

"It's true what I say. I am the good good shepherd.

"When a person is paid to look after woolly sheep, $BAAA$, they don't *really* care if the sheep, $BAAA$, are ok. They are just doing a job. And when *danger* comes like a fox, GRRRR, prowling around or a wolf, AHOOOOO, howling it's sound, the hired person just runs away!

"But the shepherd doesn't.

"The shepherd loves his sheep, $BAAA$, even if the sheep, $BAAA$, are a bit silly and do silly things like wander off and get lost! The shepherd always searches for them, cares for them and looks after them. The sheep, $BAAA$, learn to know the shepherd's voice and they know that he will keep them safe.

"I am the good good shepherd.

"Just like my Father God knows me and I know Him, I know all *my* sheep, $BAAA$. And I will lay down my life to rescue them because I love them **SOOOOO** very much.

"There are other sheep, $BAAA$, who are in far-away fields. They don't *yet* know me but I will go and look for them so they *can* be in my flock too.

"*And when danger comes* I will not run away like a hired person. But remember this...no one will take my life from me, I will give my life to rescue the sheep, $BAAA$!

"Because, I am the good good shepherd."

Have a think

Jesus described himself as the good good shepherd who would give his life for the sheep. He was starting to let people know what would soon happen to him and how he would give his life to rescue us all.

Have a go

Stick a blob of cotton wool onto a piece of paper. Now draw on a head, some legs and a woolly tail. What is your sheep, $BAAA$, going to be called?

Have a pray

Thank you, Jesus, that you are my good good shepherd. I am safe with you. Thank you that you love me, you look after me, and you even gave your life to rescue me. Amen.

Martha and Mary

Luke 10:38-42

There were two sisters who were *friends* of Jesus. One was called *Martha* and one was called *Mary*. They both *believed* in who Jesus was and in the things he said. One day they invited Jesus and his twelve friends into their home.

Martha was sorting everything out and she was BUSY, BUSY, BUSY. After all, there was a lot to do! She *brushed* the floor, she *cooked* the food, she *served* the drinks. Over and over again. BRUSH, COOK, **POUR,** *BRUSH, COOK,* **POUR,** BRUSH, COOK, **POUR**... until the floor was sparkling and Martha was EXHAUSTED!

But Mary just sat at Jesus' feet, *listening*. She *loved* to hear what he was saying. She *loved* to spend time with HER RESCUER, her friend. She *loved* feeling close to God. With eyes wide and heart alive, she could *sit there for hours.*

It wasn't long before Martha was really FED UP and huffed, "Jesus, can't you tell my sister to give me a hand! I'm doing *all* the work and she's doing n*othing!* It's not fair, this laziness should be BANNED!"

Jesus smiled kindly at Martha and said, "Martha, Martha, my friend. You're upset and worried about *so many things.* But Mary has chosen what is *really important,* for the truth in *my words* is where *true life* really begins.

"Come and spend some time with me."

Have a think

Both Martha and Mary believed in Jesus, they called him their "Lord" which means their leader, their King. But Martha was so distracted by all the things that needed to happen, she forgot what the most important thing really was… spending time with Jesus.

Have a go

Why not spend some time with Jesus. Tell him how you're feeling. Tell him what is going on in your life. Ask him what he wants to say to you.

Have a pray

Dear Jesus, I'm sorry for when I get distracted by all the things that are going on around me and the things I need to do. Please help me remember that spending time with you is the most important thing of all. Amen.

"Take this and eat. This is my body
broken for you.
Do this to remember me."

reply. The priests demanded, "Tell us the truth. Are *you* THE RESCUER, **the Son of God**?"

Jesus said, **"I AM."** The priests slapped him in the face saying, "Calling yourself God is a complete disgrace. This man should surely **DIE!"**

So, the religious leaders sent Jesus to the *Roman governor*, Pilate, for a second trial. Pilate couldn't find *anything* wrong with Jesus, because Jesus had done ***nothing wrong***.

But Pilate got "Barabbas the Murderer" and Jesus to stand in front of the crowd. Then he asked them, "*Who* do you want me to *set free*?"

The religious leaders stirred up the crowd so they all shouted, "Give *Barabbas* his liberty."

Pilate gasped, "What shall I do then with this Jesus who you call '*King*'?" and the crowd shouted back, **"Crucify, crucify crucify him!"**

So, Pilate handed Jesus over to the *soldiers*.

The soldiers WRAPPED Jesus in a purple cloak and PUSHED a crown of *sharp* thorns into his head. Then they *spat* at him and *hit* him and *mockingly* said, "Hail, King Jesus", before they took him off to the *place of the skull, the place of the dead.*

"My Father, *forgive them.*"

Then they *lifted* up the wood and left Jesus hanging on the *cross.*

It was horrible.

Mary, Jesus' mum stood at the bottom of the cross with a few other women. One of Jesus' friends, John, was also there. And they watched the one they *loved* die.

Jesus *could* have asked his Father God to save him and God *would* have. But *Jesus didn't.* He *chose* to stay on the cross so that he could rescue us all. He took a painful gasp of air and shouted, "My Father, *forgive them.*" And with his very last breath said, "It is *finished*."

Then, he bowed his head and *gave up his life.*

The sky was **BLACK**, as **BLACK AS NIGHT** even though it was the middle of the day and the soldier next to the cross, who saw how Jesus died, whispered,

"Surly this was the Son of God."

It was Friday, before the Jewish people's special day of Saturday began. So, they took his body down from the cross and placed it in a garden, in a cave. Everyone thought that everything was now over as a huge stone was rolled in front of the grave. They didn't know that ***God's great rescue plan*** was underway.

Have a think

On the cross Jesus, God's very own Son, willingly took the punishment for all the mess that gets between us and friendship with God. Jesus did this so that we can be friends with God forever. He did this because he loves us.

This was always **God's great rescue plan**.

Have a go

Tie two twigs together into the shape of a cross. Stick the cross in your tray garden, then put the big stone in front of the flowerpot cave. Remember the story isn't over yet.

Have a pray

Dear Jesus, Thank you that you love me so much that on the cross you gave up your life to rescue me. Thank you that I can now be your friend forever. Amen.

What a Sunday!

Matthew 28:1-10

ery early on the Sunday morning Jesus' friend Mary and a few other women went down to the cave where Jesus was *buried.* They were going to put perfume on Jesus' dead body and say a proper goodbye.

It was *still dark* but the *first glimmers* of *light* were peeping through the *heavy night* and a couple of birds had started to TRILL and SING.

Suddenly the air *tingled* with *wonder* and the ground began to TREMBLE and SHAKE.

The earth SHUDDERED and the DARKNESS QUAKED as the *big* stone in front of the cave was ROLLED RIGHT AWAY!

What was going on? The women were terrified. But then with a F L U T T E R and a FLAP and a B L A Z E of angel

wings an angel sat on top of the stone and said, "It's alright, **don't be afraid.** Jesus is not here he has **risen from the dead,** just like he promised he would. *Good news, good news.* THE RESCUER has *made the way* and God has well and truly *saved the day!"*

Could it be true?

The women looked into the cave. It was EMPTY! Jesus was not there! All they could do was *stand* and *stare* at the place where his lifeless body had **once** been laid. But still they didn't really understand.

Just then, JESUS himself stood right *in front* of them. He smiled and lovingly said, "Hello, it's me!" But how could this be? They had *seen* Jesus killed and now he was *filled* with life from heaven!

Mary fell at his feet and *laughed* and *cried* as she looked deep into her friend Jesus' eyes.

Jesus said, "Go and tell my disciples, *my friends* what you have seen. **Don't be afraid,** it really is me.

"I am the RESURRECTION and the LIFE for **all** *eternity."*

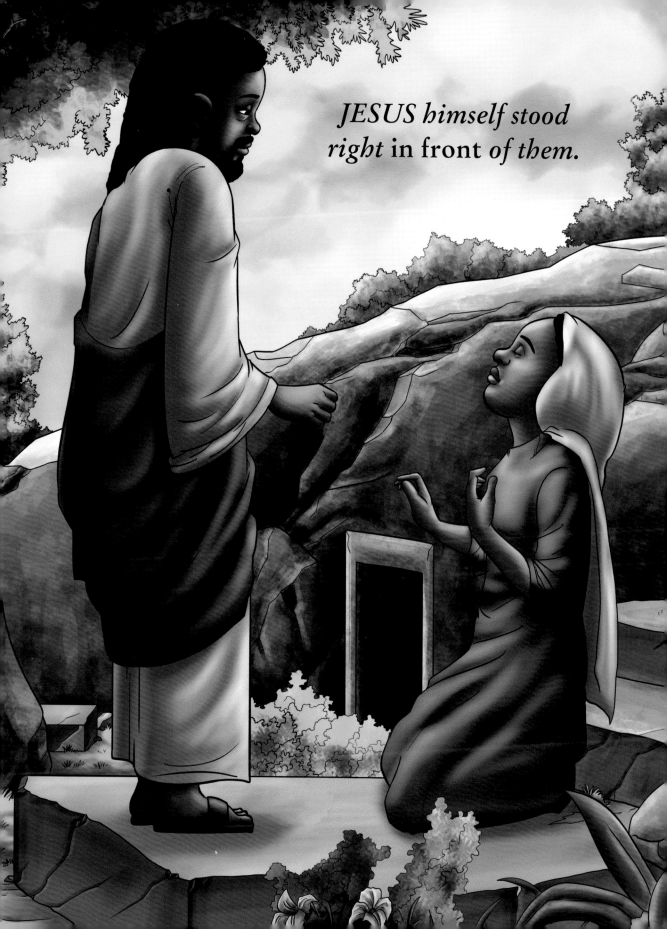

JESUS himself stood right in front of them.

Have a think

Jesus had **defeated** everything that separates us from God, even death itself. And to prove it, God raised Jesus to life again. THE RESCUER had saved the day so we can be friends with God forever. Hooray!

Have a go

On your tray garden roll the big stone in front of the cave away. Put some flowers in the garden because this first Easter morning was a day of new life and of celebration.

Have a pray

Dear Jesus, Thank you that you rose again and ended the **great separation** between God and people. Now I can have your new life in me and be your friend always.

Thank you, you are MY RESCUER. Amen.

Full of Breath

Luke 24:36-49

Jesus' special friends were very *scared*. Their knees *trembled* and their stomachs were in *knots*. They *hid* together in a room and made sure the door was completely *locked*. CLICK, CLICK, CLACK.

On Friday they had *all run away* from Jesus and now their hearts **felt broken.** Their friend was *dead and gone* and they wondered if it wouldn't be long before the religious leaders came after them.

Strangely, that morning the women had told them they'd **seen** Jesus alive by the cave. But what could it mean? The friends *didn't understand*, they *didn't believe.*

When suddenly JESUS stood in the middle of the room. From out of *nowhere*, he was suddenly *there!*

The friends gasped, "It's a Jesus ghost!" but Jesus said, "My

friends, **God's peace** to you, it's me! Give me some food to eat and you will see that I am as real as real can be."

The friends quickly gave Jesus some fish and watched him CHEW and SWALLOW it down, GULP!

They stared at Jesus with *wide eyes*, wondering if Jesus could **really** be alive. Jesus showed them his **hands** and showed them his **feet.** They could touch *the nail marks* that were now healed. They could see the *scars* of his painful death they could see he was *alive* and **full of breath!**

Jesus said, "**Peace, peace,** *my* **peace to you**. This has all happened just like I had said. 'THE RESCUER would be killed and then raised from the dead'." Then Jesus smiled the smile they knew *so* well as he laughed, "It's all been done, the RESCUE has been **won**. Now **each and everyone can be friends with God**."

They all started to laugh and then they started to cry. They giggled with glee and their hearts were alive. **Jesus had risen**, it *really* was **true.** He was THE RESCUER from God and in their hearts they *knew* that God had well and truly *saved the day.*

God *himself* **had** *made the way.*

Have a think

Jesus' friends had all deserted Jesus but Jesus still loved them. What Jesus did on the cross was for them and for all of us, to give us a fresh start with God. Jesus has rescued us from the **great separation**. Jesus' friends started the day scared but finished the day with celebration. Jesus was alive and now everything had changed.

Have a go

Take a piece of paper, roll it up into a cone shape and stick it together. Decorate it with sparkles and streamers to turn it into a party hat. Then, why not put on some music and have a dance to celebrate that Jesus is alive!

Have a pray

Dear Jesus, Thank you that because of what you did on the cross we can all have a fresh start with God. Thank you, Jesus, that you are alive and that you are THE RESCUER! Amen.

God With Us

Matthew 28:16-20

Later on Jesus' friends went up a mountain in Galilee and there they met Jesus again.

Their *hearts* were BURSTING with **joy** as they saw their *friend*, as they saw God's *special SON*. God's great rescue plan was underway, THE RESCUER **had come!**

Jesus said them to them, "You are my friends and you have seen it all with your own eyes and touched it all with your own hands. Now you are a *part* of *God's great love story,* you are *part* of **God's great rescue plans.**

"So, *go* and *tell* everyone the **whole world** over! *Tell* them everything you have heard and seen. *Tell* them that I LOVE them and they can be FRIENDS with God. *Tell* them their hearts can be washed CLEAN. *Tell* them that **whoever** believes

and trusts in me can have NEW LIFE for NOW and all ETERNITY."

Jesus promised his friends that one day he would come back again. And in a blaze of heaven's glory, Jesus went back up into heaven saying, "Don't be afraid. **I am with you** always by my Holy Spirit. I will *never* leave you on your own.

"Know that **I am with you** to the very END OF THE AGE."

Have a think

God is always with us. Jesus promised to never leave us on our own. He is with us every second, every hour, every day. And he has a part for us to play in his great love story, his great rescue plans.

Have a go

Is there someone that you could tell the good news of Jesus to?

Have a pray

Dear Jesus, Thank you that you are always with me and you love me. Thank you that I am your friend. Thank you that you want to use me in your great rescue plans. Amen.

And Then...

The book of Acts and onwards

After Jesus went back to heaven he gave the gift of the *Holy Spirit* to his friends so they would always know that *God was close to them*. And when they received the Holy Spirit in their hearts, they became brave.

They went *the **whole world** over* TELLING people about Jesus THE RESCUER. HEALING people in Jesus' name and BAPTISING them in the name of the Father, the Son and the Holy Spirit.

From then on many, many, many more people became Jesus' friends and are still becoming his friends to this very day.

If you would like to be Jesus' friend you can pray this prayer.

Jesus will hear and he will be your *friend always*.

Dear Jesus,

Thank you that you love me. Thank you that you died to rescue me.
Thank you that you rose again.
I'm sorry for anything I have done that has come between us
being friends.
Please forgive me and wash my heart clean.

I believe in you. Please come and be the leader of my life.
Please come and be my friend.

Thank you that you are THE RESCUER who is with me,
Now and always.

Amen.